William Frank Eugene Gurley

Bulletin No. 4 of the Illinois State Museum of Natural History

Upper Devonian and Niagara Crinoids

William Frank Eugene Gurley

Bulletin No. 4 of the Illinois State Museum of Natural History
Upper Devonian and Niagara Crinoids

ISBN/EAN: 9783743443174

Manufactured in Europe, USA, Canada, Australia, Japa

Cover: Foto ©ninafisch / pixelio.de

Manufactured and distributed by brebook publishing software
(www.brebook.com)

William Frank Eugene Gurley

Bulletin No. 4 of the Illinois State Museum of Natural History

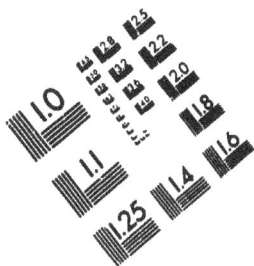

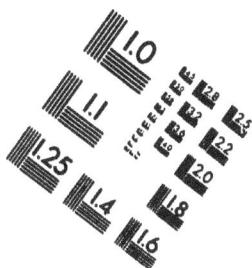

**IMAGE EVALUATION
TEST TARGET (MT-3)**

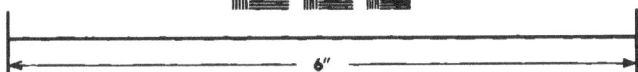

|← 6" →|

Photographic
Sciences
Corporation

23 WEST MAIN STREET
WEBSTER, N.Y. 14580
(716) 572-4503

Technical and Bibliographic Notes/Notes techniques et bibliographiques

The Institute has attempted to obtain the best original copy available for filming. Features of this copy which may be bibliographically unique, which may alter any of the images in the reproduction, or which may significantly change the usual method of filming, are checked below.

L'Institut a microfilmé le meilleur exemplaire qu'il lui a été possible de se procurer. Les détails de cet exemplaire qui sont peut-être uniques du point de vue bibliographique, qui peuvent modifier une image reproduite, ou qui peuvent exiger une modification dans la méthode normale de filmage sont indiqués ci-dessous.

☐ Coloured covers/
Couverture de couleur

☐ Covers damaged/
Couverture endommagée

☐ Covers restored and/or laminated/
Couverture restaurée et/ou pelliculée

☐ Cover title missing/
Le titre de couverture manque

☐ Coloured maps/
Cartes géographiques en couleur

☐ Coloured ink (i.e. other than blue or black)/
Encre de couleur (i.e. autre que bleue ou noire)

☐ Coloured plates and/or illustrations/
Planches et/ou illustrations en couleur

☐ Bound with other material/
Relié avec d'autres documents

☐ Tight binding may cause shadows or distortion along interior margin/
La reliure serrée peut causer de l'ombre ou de la distortion le long de la marge intérieure

☐ Blank leaves added during restoration may appear within the text. Whenever possible, these have been omitted from filming/
Il se peut que certaines pages blanches ajoutées lors d'une restauration apparaissent dans le texte, mais, lorsque cela était possible, ces pages n'ont pas été filmées.

☐ Additional comments:/
Commentaires supplémentaires:

☐ Coloured pages/
Pages de couleur

☐ Pages damaged/
Pages endommagées

☐ Pages restored and/or laminated/
Pages restaurées et/ou pelliculées

☑ Pages discoloured, stained or foxed/
Pages décolorées, tachetées ou piquées

☐ Pages detached/
Pages détachées

☑ Showthrough/
Transparence

☐ Quality of print varies/
Qualité inégale de l'impression

☐ Includes supplementary material/
Comprend du matériel supplémentaire

☐ Only edition available/
Seule édition disponible

☐ Pages wholly or partially obscured by errata slips, tissues, etc., have been refilmed to ensure the best possible image/
Les pages totalement ou partiellement obscurcies par un feuillet d'errata, une pelure, etc., ont été filmées à nouveau de façon à obtenir la meilleure image possible.

The images appearing here are the best quality possible considering the condition and legibility of the original copy and in keeping with the filming contract specifications.

Original copies in printed paper covers are filmed beginning with the front cover and ending on the last page with a printed or illustrated impression, or the back cover when appropriate. All other original copies are filmed beginning on the first page with a printed or illustrated impression, and ending on the last page with a printed or illustrated impression.

The last recorded frame on each microfiche shall contain the symbol →► (meaning "CONTINUED"), or the symbol ▽ (meaning "END"), whichever applies.

Maps, plates, charts, etc., may be filmed at different reduction ratios. Those too large to be entirely included in one exposure are filmed beginning in the upper left hand corner, left to right and top to bottom, as many frames as required. The following diagrams illustrate the method:

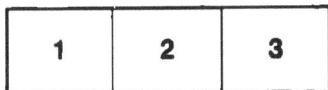

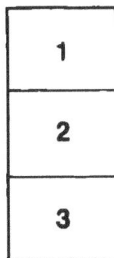

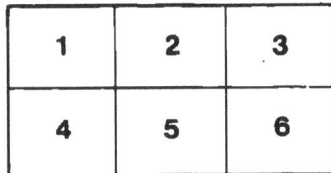

Les images suivantes ont été reproduites avec le plus grand soin, compte tenu de la condition et de la netteté de l'exemplaire filmé, et en conformité avec les conditions du contrat de filmage.

Les exemplaires originaux dont la couverture en papier est imprimée sont filmés en commençant par le premier plat et en terminant soit par la dernière page qui comporte une empreinte d'impression ou d'illustration, soit par le second plat, selon le cas. Tous les autres exemplaires originaux sont filmés en commençant par la première page qui comporte une empreinte d'impression ou d'illustration et en terminant par la dernière page qui comporte une telle empreinte.

Un des symboles suivants apparaîtra sur la dernière image de chaque microfiche, selon le cas: le symbole →► signifie "A SUIVRE", le symbole ▽ signifie "FIN".

Les cartes, planches, tableaux, etc., peuvent être filmés à des taux de réduction différents. Lorsque le document est trop grand pour être reproduit en un seul cliché, il est filmé à partir de l'angle supérieur gauche, de gauche à droite, et de haut en bas, en prenant le nombre d'images nécessaire. Les diagrammes suivants illustrent la méthode.

1	2	3

1
2
3

1	2	3
4	5	6

BULLETIN NO. 4

OF THE

ILLINOIS STATE MUSEUM

OF

NATURAL HISTORY.

UPPER DEVONIAN AND NIAGARA CRINOIDS.

By S. A. MILLER and Wm. F. E. GURLEY.

SPRINGFIELD, ILLINOIS,
October 15, 1894.

SPRINGFIELD, ILL.
ED F HARTMAN, STATE PRINTER,
1894.

ILLINOIS STATE MUSEUM

OF

NATURAL HISTORY,

SPRINGFIELD, ILLINOIS.

SUBKINGDOM ECHINODERMATA.

CLASS CRINOIDEA.
ORDER PALÆOCRINOIDEA.
FAMILY MELOCRINIDÆ.

DOLATOCRINUS MAGNIFICUS, n. sp.

Plate 1, Fig. 1, basal view of the calyx, injured in the middle part; Fig. 2, view of the vault, part of which is broken away and the sutures between the plates only partly preserved; Fig. 3, lateral view, with the six-armed ray in front and showing height of vault.

Calyx very large sub-hemispheroidal, broadly lobed in the radial fields and slightly concave below. The radial field opposite the azygous side is much larger, more prominent and more broadly lobed than either of the others. The diameter of the specimen illustrated is two and six-tenths inches and height one and two-tenths inches. The dome is only moderately convex, the radial areas being raised and the interradial areas depressed. Surface of the plates of the calyx sculptured, the larger ones bearing a central node. The radiating ridges do not connect from one plate to another, as is usual in the ornamentation of crinoids, but a radiating ridge may be directed toward the suture between two adjoining plates, instead of joining an end to that of a similar ridge on a contiguous plate; and there are shorter and longer ridges and nodes on the plates. The plates of a kind, however, are ornamented alike and on the whole the ornamentation is very pleasing.

The column, in our specimen, is broken off by an irregular fracture and part of the radial plates are injured. Enough is preserved, however, to show that the column is very large and conceals the basal plates that are deeply sunken in the interior of the calyx. The columnar canal is slightly pentalobate.

Basal plates concealed in the calyx. First primary radials probably as long as wide, including the projection up into the calyx to reach the basal plates, but one-half wider than high as exposed around the columnar cavity. The superior side of each is quite concave, and the inferior end is abruptly sunk in the basal cavity, so as to form a funnel around the upper end of the column, as we have seen in specimens of *D. marshi* and other species in this genus, but the depth of the funnel we have not observed in this species.

Second primary radials quadrangular, one-third wider than high, both the inferior and superior sides somewhat convex, and each bears a rather large central tubercle. The superior sides of these plates curve slightly upward and the inferior sides bend a little toward the basal depression, so that the calyx may be made to rest on the central tubercles of these plates.

Third primary radials, in four of the rays, pentagonal, larger than the second radials and about one-fourth wider than long. We will follow these four rays to the arms and afterward recur to the other ray. On each of the upper sloping sides of these four third primary radials there is a single, large, hexagonal, secondary radial, which supports on each of its superior sides two tertiary radials, the last of which supports the free arms. This gives us four arms to each of these four radial series.

In the other or fifth ray, which is opposite the azygous area, the third primary radial is broadly truncated above, hexagonal, twice as wide as high, and supports, upon its upper face, a series of three intersecondary and intertertiary plates, and upon each of its superior lateral sides a single large secondary radial, one of which is hexagonal and the other heptagonal. Each secondary radial bears upon its inner superior sloping side a series of three tertiary radials, the last one of which bears a free arm, and upon its outer superior sloping side a single, large, tertiary radial, which, in turn, supports upon each of its two upper sloping sides two radials of the fourth or quarternary series, the last of which support free arms. This structure gives to this ray six arms. The first intersecondary radial in this series is a large, quadrangular plate, having nearly equal sides; it is followed by an hexagonal plate abutting its two undersloping sides upon the secondary radials and two upper sloping sides upon the tertiary radials and supporting upon the upper truncated face a somewhat smaller pentagonal plate, that abuts its superior sloping sides against the adjacent tertiary radials, that support the free arms. The six plates that support the six free arms in this radial series abut against each other without any intervening plates.

There are, as shown above, twenty-two arms, in this species, which are more than have been found in any species heretofore described. If, however, the ray containing six arms and three interradial plates is abnormal the species would have twenty arms and still be so different from any species heretofore described that no comparison with any of them would serve any purpose in distinguishing it. There is nothing to indicate that this six-armed radial series may be abnormal and we believe it is in the normal condition of the species.

The first interradials are the larger plates of the calyx as exposed on the surface, and larger, in fact, than any of the other plates, unless the first primary radials, including that part which forms the funnel in the columnar cavity should prove to have as great or greater size. The one opposite the six-armed series or first azygous interradial is the larger one and has eleven sides; an approximate one is the smaller and has nine sides; the other three have ten sides each. The first interradial is followed by a single plate that extends nearly to the top of the calyx, and which, in turn, is followed by one or two small plates that separate the arms and connect with the plates of the vault, except in the azygous area, where three plates separate the arms and connect with the plates of the vault. The sutures between the plates in the upper part of some of the interradial areas are not distinct in our specimen, and for that reason are not shown in the illustration.

The dome or vault, as may be seen in the illustration, has part of the plates broken away on the azygous side and some of the sutures are anchylosed or obscure. It is, however, covered with large, polygonal plates of very unequal size. It is most convex toward the six-armed series opposite the azygous side and most sinuate or depressed at the azygous interradius. No pores or passages through the vault between the arms have been found in our specimen.

The specimen from which the foregoing description is drawn is the largest known Dolatocrinus. It was found in the Hamilton Group, at the Falls of the Ohio, and is now in the collection of Wm. F. E. Gurley.

8

DOLATOCRINUS SPINOSUS n. sp.

Plate I, Fig. 4, basal view of the calyx, without the surface mark-
ings of the plates; Fig. 5, lateral view, showing some
of the spines on the plates of the vault.

Calyx large, subhemispheroidal, broadly lobed in the radial fields,
and depressed concave on the lower side. Apparently no azygous
interradius. The diameter of the specimen illustrated is two and
two-tenths inches, and height three-fourths of an inch, though we
have seen specimens only about two-thirds as large. Vault moderately
convex and slightly depressed in the interradial areas. A strong
ridge crosses the primary radials. Column round and deeply inserted in the calyx. Surface ornamentation not preserved in any
of our specimens.

Basal plates sunk deep within the calyx and extending internally
as high as the arm openings. First primary radials twice as wide
as high externally, but near the middle of the plates they are
abruptly bent, almost at right angles, into the basal cavity, where
they form a funnel to the basal plates, into which the column is
inserted, so that, in fact, their length is fully equal to their greatest width. The superior face is slightly concave.

Second primary radials quadrangular and more than one-half
wider than high. Third primary radials slightly larger than the
second, pentagonal, a little wider than high, and supporting upon
each upper sloping side a single secondary radial.

Secondary radials nearly as large as the third primary radials
pentagonal, and supporting upon each upper sloping side a series
of three tertiary radials, the last one of which bears the free arms.
The first tertiary radials are larger than the second or third. The
species bears twenty arms.

The first interradials, in each area, are elongated eleven sided
plates and larger than any of the other plates in the body. Each
one is followed by an hexagonal plate that is as long or longer than
wide and supports three narrow, elongated plates in the third
range that reach as high as the base of the arms. These are followed, in the fourth range, by three plates that separate the arms,
and unite with the plates of the vault. One or two intersecondary plates (apparently a pair of them) are inserted at the base of
the arms in the intersecondary areas, but it is not clear, in our

specimens, that they unite with the plates of the vault. Probably
they do not, but as the sutures are destroyed this cannot be determined.

The limestone matrix covers the greater part of the vault, in
our best specimen, so that but little can be said of it beyond what
is shown by the illustration. It is characterized, however, by a
plate over each double radial series which bears a very long, strong
spine. The broken ends of spines belonging to other plates are
preserved in the matrix, but there is no evidence of a proboscis.
The summit of the vault is apparently below the top of the matrix
shown in the illustration, and not as high as the top of the spines
over the radial series.

There have been described, heretofore, only two species bearing twenty arms— *D. lamellosus* and *D. troosti*—and this species
is so far removed from them that comparison is unnecessary.

Found in the Hamilton Group, at Charleston, Indiana, and now
in the collection of Wm. F. E. Gurley.

DOLATOCRINUS LACUS, Lyon.

Plate 1, Fig. 6, side view; Fig. 7, basal view.

Lyon described the body as "subglobose, truncated below, columnar pit broad and deep; summit somewhat conical, prolonged
by a proboscis: column round, columnar perforation rather large
and pentalobate." He said; "The body is adorned by a most
beautiful network of raised triangular figures; the points of the
principal triangular figures rise from, and terminate at the center
of the first interradial pieces; a subordinate set of figures terminate
at the center of all the pieces below the arms. In some specimens the lines are continuous, in others, interrupted. The summit pieces are sometimes adorned by a single prominent granule;
in other specimens, many of the pieces are ornamented by a number of granules, arranged in lines across some of the pieces in
nearly parallel rows, or in a circular band around a more prominent central one."

Our specimens agree with the above description and in comparison with other species we would note the high calyx, with a slight
constriction below the arm bases, the flattened or truncated base,
and pentagonal, funnel shaped, columnar pit, bounded externally

—2 G.

by a raised ridge running from a central tubercle on each first radial to another, so as to bound the columnar cavity with a raised pentagonal figure. We have illustrated a basal view to show this pentagonal outline, because Lyon's figure does not show its pentagonal character.

The basal plates are deeply sunken. First primary radials including the extension into the columnar cavity longer than wide; ornamented with sculptured ridges, which terminate at a central node, at each angle of the columnar depression. Second radials quandrangular, wider than high, and bearing a central node. Third radials pentagonal, wider than high, and bearing a central node. First secondary radials as large or larger than the third primary radials. Second secondary radials much smaller and of irregular form and size. Third secondary radials still smaller and of irregular form and size. Arms, ten, composed of ovoid flat pieces of equal thickness.

First interradials the larger plates of the calyx, nine-sided, subovate, angularly pointed below and resting between the upper sloping sides of the first primary radials, the upper sloping sides separate the first secondary radials and the superior side is truncated for a single plate in the second range. Second interradials subquadrate, four pentagonal and one quandrangular and followed by two small plates in the third range (in some areas there are three) and these by three smaller, elongated plates (sometimes there are only two) that separate the arms and unite with the plates of the vault. Intersecondary plates, two, similar to the last three in the interradial areas, and separating the arm bases and uniting with the plates of the vault. Above the summit of the three intersecondary plates and also above the summit of the last two or three interradials, two elongated pores or passages penetrate the vault horizontally. In some interradial areas there are four of these pores, especially where there are three plates in the third range. These pores are conspicuous, in our specimens, but they seem to have been entirely overlooked by Lyon, for they are not shown in his illustration or mentioned in his text. We have given a side view of a specimen for the purpose of showing the interradials and intersecondary plates and the pores, because Lyon's illustration is very erroneous and defective, in all these respects.

Found in the Upper Helderberg Group, at the Falls of the Ohio, and in Clark County, Indiana.

DOLATOCRINUS MARSHII, Lyon.

Plate 1, Fig. 8, showing the abrupt bending of the first radials into a pentagonal funnel shaped cavity.

This species was described and illustrated, by Lyon, in 1869, in the Transactions of the American Philosophical Society, vol. XIII, p. 461, pl. XXVII, Figs. *n, n1 and n2.* His description and illustrations are very good, and for the purpose of identifying the species none other are necessary, but that publication is rare and but few western people ever have an opportunity to see it, and, for that reason alone, we are justified in redescribing it. But our principal object, in calling attention to it, is for the purpose of redescribing and showing a basal view, as we have a specimen hollow on the inside and showing both the exterior and interior of all the plates.

Lyon described the calyx as "discoid, with five broad, sharp carina, which rise perpendicularly from the margin of the basal pit, and extend outward, equally elevated to the center of the third radials, the carina rising gradually from the margins of the radials, then more rapidly to the center of the pieces. At the center of the third radials the carina sends out branches, not quite so bold as the main stem, but strong, involving all the pieces of the superradials up to the arm bases. Arm bases prominent, in groups of two to each ray, producing a lobed, pentagonal figure of that section of the body. The dome is subconical; twice as high as the body below the arms; surmounted by a thick, strong, subcentral proboscis. The interradial fields unite to the dome-covering between the arms."

The characters above described, to which special attention may be directed, are the low calyx, high vault, subcentral proboscis and carina. Instead of ordinary radial ridges occupying the central part of the radial plates, the whole plates are involved in forming a high central ridge, in each series, which Lyon calls the "carina." And they "rise perpendicularly from the margin of the basal point," which is a striking peculiarity, much more noticeable in a specimen than it is in his illustration or in ours, though the attention of the artist was called specially to it, and our figure is accurate except in giving a full idea of the height of the "carina" at the "basal pit." The surface of the plates is covered with fine ridges, disposed in groups, radiating from the center of the plates.

The basal plates form a cone, the top of which is on a level with the top of the calyx. The internal position which they occupied, probably caused them to become anchylosed, at all events, one cannot see any possible flexibility they could give the animal, in that situation, if they were not anchylosed. The summit of these anchylosed plates is perforated with a large pentalobate or cinque-foil columnar canal. There is a rim, formed by a thickening of the plates, within the apical part of the cone to which the end of the column was attached, and it appears that the column filled the interior of the cone and the plates were more or less attached to it.

The first primary radials form a pentagonal funnel that extends to the base of the cone formed by the basal plates. The length of the funnel, without including the height of the carina, is equal to the greatest width of the radials. In other words, the length of the first radials is more than their greatest width, but the plates are abruptly bent, and four-fifths of the length is within the funnel shaped basal cavity, and only one-fifth without, which is very little more than the thickness of a plate. It seems quite impossible to show the true depth of the funnel, by pen drawing, but the artist has indicated it as well as he could, in the illustration, which is a character not attempted to be shown, in Lyon's figure of the base of the calyx of this species. In the inside of the calyx, neither the pentagonal form of the funnel nor the external carina are indicated, but a round cone is formed by the extension into the interior of the first radials and basal plates.

Second primary radials quadrangular one-half wider than long. Third primary radials wider than the second and wider than long, pentagonal, and support on each upper sloping side three or four secondary radials, the last of which supports the free arms. The radial series are of variable length within the calyx, as mentioned by Lyon, which somewhat destroys the symmetry of the calyx. There are ten arms.

There are from seven to nine interradials in each area. The first is large, subovoid and has nine sides, it supports a hexagonal plate as large as a primary radial, and it is followed by three plates, in the third range, except in one area, where there are only two. There are two plates in the fourth range, except in one area, where there are four, and two in the fifth range, to which are united the points of the long pieces that lie between the lobes on the dome, according to Lyon. Some specimens, however, we think show more than two plates, in the last range, in some of the areas.

There are from two to four intersecondary plates in each area wedged between the arm bases; when four, they are in pairs, one above the other.

"The dome is covered by large pieces; each field between the lobes contains a pair of the largest, which reach from the arm-bases toward the proboscis; they are six or seven sided; long; broadest at the upper extremity; pointed, or very slightly truncated at the lower end; joining each other by their longest sides, at the center of the depression between the lobes. A circle of large pieces surround the dome; all of these rest partly upon the ten long pieces. The pieces composing this zone are of different sizes; they also differ in form; all six sided; two of the largest pieces of the circle rest directly over two of the long pieces; three other groups of the long pieces unite under the suture, uniting two of the pieces forming the circle, so that the sutures, uniting both sets of pieces, form one line from the arm bases to the base of the second circle surrounding the dome near the base of the proboscis. Below the zone described, and between the groups of long pieces, are groups of from five to seven pieces, the upper one of which is joined to the circle above the group of long pieces, and on which it rests. The lowest piece of these groups is lanceolate; is lodged between the arm bases, and unites with the interbrachials. The upper and largest piece of these several groups is of the same size and form as the pieces comprising the first zone around the top of the dome. Around the arm bases the pieces are numerous and quite small. The pieces comprising the lower zone, and the large ones of the groups above the arms, are surmounted by a group of from three to five rough, pointed spines, confluent near their bases. The plates of the second zone at the base of the proboscis are ornamented with hemispherical tubercles, all other pieces of the dome are gibbous or concave and not ornamented."

In this species there are from four to six pores between each of the arm bases, that were not mentioned by Lyon, or shown in his illustrations, and which are quite conspicuous in our specimens. These pores or passages are elongated. They commence by a slight horizontal furrow across the top of the last interradial plates in the calyx and penetrate the adjoining plates of the vault horizontally, which makes an elongated surface opening. This feature is present and even more noticeable in *Dolatocrinus grandis* and may be understood by referring to the illustration of that species. We know all these openings penetrate the test because we can see through them.

This species occurs in the Upper Helderburg Group, at the Falls of the Ohio, and in Clark county, Indiana.

DOLATOCRINUS GRANDIS, n. sp.

Plate II, Fig. 1, basal view of the calyx; Fig. 2, view of the vault broken in the central part; Fig. 3, lateral view.

Calyx very large, subhemispheroidal, quite concave below, the concavity including part of the third primary plates, and most depressed in the interradial areas. The diameter of the specimen illustrated is two and three-tenths inches; height to the place where the vault is broken, one and fifty-five hundredths inches; height of calyx, nine-tenths of an inch; height of vault, if unbroken, and calyx about equal. The vault is quite convex, a little more abrupt on one side than the other, indicating that it possessed a proboscis on the abrupt side, and it is very slightly depressed in the interradial areas. Surface of the calyx beautifully and delicately sculptured, numerous raised lines seem to cross the sutures from one plate to another, but none of them arise from nodes or tubercles. The sutures are not beveled and in some parts they are very indistinct. The sutures on the vault are distinct and beveled and between the larger plates they are broadly and deeply grooved, the grooves being bounded with a rim of granules, while the central part of each plate is concave or sculptured and sometimes granulous. The columnar cavity and part of the first primary radials, in our specimen, are covered with the limestone matrix.

First primary radials very little wider than high, upper side transverse. Second primary radials quadrangular and about one-fourth wider than high. Third primary radials larger than the second, pentagonal, and from one-fourth to one-third wider than

high. The superior sides bend upward and the inferior sides curve
into the basal depression so that the calyx can be made to rest
on a smooth surface on the third radials. Each one supports on
each upper sloping side a series of secondary radials the last ones
of which support the free arms.

The first secondary radials are fully as large or larger than the
third primary radials, rather wider than high, part of them pentagonal and the others hexagonal, and each one abuts upon the
first interradial and one of the plates in the second range of interradials. The second secondary radials are as large as the first
and wider than high, but not of uniform size. The third secondary
radials seem to be smaller than the second, but the sutures are
anchylosed, or so obscure, in our specimen, that the outlines cannot be accurately determined. Above these the arm bases become prominent. There are only ten arms in this species, but
they are very large and composed of a double series of interlocking plates.

The interradial areas are not exactly of uniform size nor is it
certain that they are filled with the same number of plates. The
first interradials are the larger plates in the calyx. Each one has
ten sides, is much elongated, rests its lower angle between the two
upper sloping sides of two first primary radials, and separates the
first secondary radials between its upper lateral sides, and supports upon the two superior faces two rather large and more or
less elongated plates in the second range. In some areas these
plates are larger than in other areas. In three of the areas, where
the sutures are distinct, there are two plates, in the third range,
about half the size of those in the second range, four small plates
in the fourth range, six still smaller plates in the fifth range, and
eight small plates in the sixth range, that form the top of the
calyx between the arm bases and unite with the plates of the
vault, in a zig zag line. Whether or not the plates in the other
two areas are the same cannot be determined from our specimen.

The intersecondary areas are short, but almost like the interradial areas, in the upper part, and the plates consist of four
ranges. The first one, consisting of two plates, rests between the
upper slightly sloping sides of the second secondary radials and
in line with the third range of interradials; it is followed by four
plates in the second range, six in the third range and eight in the
fourth range, that unite with the plates of the vault, in a zig zag

line. The sutures are so obscure between the small plates, in some of the areas, that it cannot be determined whether or not all the areas are exactly alike. The arms are separated about equally distant from each other, whether by the interradials or intersecondary radials.

There seems to be no azygous area in the calyx.

The vault, in our specimen, as may be seen in the illustration, is broken away at the summit. It is, however, highly convex, the convexity probably equalling the height of the calyx, and covered with ornamented polygonal plates arranged in peculiar and systematic order. The sutures are distinct, even between the smaller plates, and the edges of the plates are beveled, and between the larger plates the sutures are widely grooved. The plates are depressed convex, concave in the center and more or less sculptured and granulous. The smaller plates are over the arm furrows and regularly interlock. The plates toward the central area are large and polygonal. The plates in the interradial areas are elongated and arranged fan like, in some of the areas, and more like a keystone arch in others, which have a very long, wedge shaped plate in the middle. There are eight or ten plates in each depressed interradial area. A horizontal furrow crosses the top of each of the last plates of the calyx and penetrates the vault at the suture between the plates of the interradial areas. There are, therefore, eight or ten horizontal elongated pores or passages that penetrate the vault between each of the arms. They are shown in the illustration. This subject will be further considered in remarks at the close of the descriptions of *Dolatocrinus* in this article.

Found in the Hamilton Group, at Louisville, Ky., and now in the collection of Wm. F. E. Gurley.

DOLATOCRINUS ORNATUS *var*. ASPERATUS, n. *var*.

Plate 11, Fig. 4, basal view, Fig. 5, view of the vault; Fig. 6, side view.

Calyx low, basin shaped, flattened or truncated at the base as far as the extent of the second radials; columnar cavity small; primary radial ridges prominent; surface of all the plates closely and radiately sculptured and pitted.

Basal plates hidden by the column, which is round and pierced with a cinque-foil canal. First primary radials longer than wide and only a small part at the lower end is curved into the columnar cavity. Strong radial ridges rise on the first radials, cross the second and terminate at a tubercle on the third radials, from which a delicate ridge crosses each secondary radial. The radial ridges are most prominent in the central part of the plates. The radiating lines from the commencement of the radiating ridges form a pentagonal figure around the small columnar cavity. Second primary radials quadrangular and wider than long. Third primary radials larger than the second, wider than high, pentagonal and support on each upper sloping side two secondary radials.

First secondary radials about as large as the third primary radials and hexagonal, except in some instances, where slightly truncated by a small plate resting between the upper lateral side of the second interradial and the base of the arm, they become heptagonal. Second secondary radials much smaller; they separate the arms and extend to the summit of the calyx and slope laterally. There are ten arms, composed, at their origin, of a double series of plates. No intersecondary radials.

The first interradials are the larger plates of the body and have nine sides. The second interradials are less than half as large as the first and hexagonal; the three superior sides are the shorter ones; the upper truncated side extends to the summit of the calyx and a small vault plate abuts laterally against it. A small plate rests between each superior lateral side and the second secondary radial and forms part of the support of the free arm. There is no azygous area.

The vault is only slightly convex and very much depressed in the interradial areas, especially between the arm bases. It bears a small subcentral proboscis that is not preserved in our specimens. It is covered with rather large, polygonal, tuberculated plates, two of which, in each depressed interradial space, are elongated, and the larger plates of the vault. There are no pores or passages that penetrate the vault between the arms.

Found in the Hamilton Group, near Charleston, Indiana, and now in the collection of Wm. F. E. Gurley.

DOLATOCRINUS ORNATUS, Meek.

*Plate II, Fig. 7, basal view; Fig. 8, summit view; Fig. 9, side
view of the same specimen from Columbus, Ohio.*

The following is the definition of this species, by Meek, from
the Proceedings of the Academy of Natural Sciences of Philadel-
phia, 1871. p. 57. It has never, before, been illustrated.

"Body including the vault, depressed subglobose, the portion
below the arm bases being a little higher than the vault, with
nearly vertical sides above, but rounding under below to the somewhat flattened under side; arm bases protuberant, mainly in con-
sequence of the rather deep furrows or sinuses of the vault over
the interradial areas; vault composed of irregular pieces, each of
which projects in the form of a little sharply prominent node or
short spine, the largest of which are situated around the nearly
central ventral tube, and on the elevations between it and the arm
bases. Base small, a little compressed within the shallow concavity of the under side, and marked by a distinctly indented column-
facet, which occupies near three-fourths of its entire breadth, so
that only a narrow ring, as it were, of the basal pieces can be
seen when the column is attached. First radial pieces comparatively large, extending out nearly horizontally, or only a little
arching upward, and with their inner ends curving slightly into
the shallow central concavity; all wider than long, and hexagonal,
with the upper (outer) side of each longer than any of the others.
Second radial pieces about half as large as the first, wider than
long, and quadrangular in outline. (In one ray of the typical
specimen the second radial is abnormally wanting, while the third
is larger than usual.) Third radials about as large as the second,
from the curved-up edges of which they rise vertically wider than
long, and pentagonal in form; bearing on each of their superior
sloping sides a smaller secondary radial, each of which supports
another smaller, more or less cuneiform piece, from which the
arms arise; thus making two arms from each ray, unless the number is increased by bifurcations after they become free; arms
unknown, but apparently composed, at their origin, of a double
series of alternating pieces.

"First interradial pieces, somewhat larger than the first radials,
about as wide above the middle as their length, eight or nine
sided, with the lower part of each curving under to connect with

the first radials, while they curve upward vertically from near or below the middle; each supporting on the upper side a much smaller hexagonal piece, which rises vertically, and usually bears on its short superior lateral edges two smaller pieces connecting with the secondary radials or first arm-pieces, while its short truncated upper side is not surmounted by any succeeding piece, but connects on its inner surface with the vault.

"Sutures between all the plates channeled. Surface of body plates ornamented with raised lines or very small radiating costæ, that cross the sutures parallel to each other at the sides of the plates, but soon become bent about and connected, in various ways, so that very few of them extend directly to the middle of any of the plates, the arrangement being such as to produce a kind of vermicular style of ornamentation, especially over all the central part of the plates, like that often seen on the body plates in *Amphoracrinus*. A small rather sharp ridge also extends up the middle of each radial series of plates, more or less interrupted at the sutures, and showing a slight tendency to form a pinched node on the middle of the first and second radials; while it is sometimes seen to bifurcate on the third radial, to send branches to the secondary radials, but these are generally so small as scarcely to be distinguished from the other little ridges ornamenting all of the body pieces.

"Ventral tube unknown, but judging from the spiniferous character of the vault-pieces around its base, probably also spiniferous.

"Height of body to arm-bases, 0.47 inch. do. to top of vault, 0.60 inch; breadth, 0.95 inch."

The specimen illustrated is from the typical locality, in the Upper Helderburg Group, at Columbus, Ohio, and is from the collection of Charles Faber. It will be observed that it is about the size of the type described by Meek, and agrees with it in all particulars. The variety *asperatus*, above described, has a proportionally longer calyx, which produces some difference in the relative sizes of the plates, but this alone would not be of varietal importance; taken, however, in connection with the different surface ornamentation and the great difference in the ridges that cross the radial plates, varietal characters may exist. The plates on the superior lateral sides of the second interradials are proportionally smaller in *D. ornatus* than in *D. ornatus var. asperatus* and other minor differences might be pointed out, but they do not seem to us to constitute specific differences, though the two forms on cursory examination are readily separated. If the arms were preserved possibly the two forms could be specifically distinguished.

DOLATOCRINUS STELLIFER n. sp.

Plate II, Fig. 10, basal view; Fig. 11, view of the vault, only part
of the sutures can be distinguished and the ornamenta-
tion is not preserved; Fig. 12, internal view of
the calyx showing the basal plates and
part of the first primary radials.

Calyx low, basin shaped, three time as wide as high, deeply and broadly concave below, the concavity extending to the middle of the first interradials; columnar cavity deep; radial ridges quite small. Surface of all the plates deeply, closely and radiately sculptured.

Basal plates extending in a cylindrical form up as high as the top of the calyx and completely hidden externally by the column, which fills the cylindrical area. The column is round and pierced with a cinque-foil canal. First primary radials longer than wide and together forming a funnel-shaped columnar cavity, ornamented near the top with two raised lines, forming a pentagon, with a furrow between them. Second primary radials a little wider than high, quadrangular, gradually expanding upward, and each orna-mented with a small, sharp radial ridge that rises at an angle of the pentagonal ornamentation, on the first radial, and, crossing the second and third radial bifurcates at the superior angle of the third radial, from which point a broken ridge crosses each second-ary radial series to the free arms. On each side of the radial ridges the plates are closely, deeply and radiately sculptured. Third primary radials shorter than the second, pentagonal, expanding up-ward to the lateral angles and supporting on each upper sloping side a secondary radial series.

There are four secondary radials in each of nine series, and they become smaller toward the arms, which commence, at the arm openings, with a double series of interlocking plates. They are radiately sculptured from a more or less well defined central node. One secondary radial series in our specimen consists of a single pen-tagonal plate which bears upon each of the upper sloping sides a tertiary radial series having three plates before reaching the double series of interlocking plates, at the base of the arms. There are, therefore, eleven arms composed at their bases of a double series of interlocking plates.

The first interradials are the larger plates of the body and have nine sides. They are deeply stellate in their ornamentation. The second interradials are more than twice as wide as high and apparently heptagonal as the two superior sloping sides of each appear to bear four small plates that separate the second and third secondary radials. These plates are followed by two plates that separate the fourth secondary radials, and upon the superior lateral sides of these plates there is a single small plate, on the side of the arm base, that appears to properly belong to the calyx. There are, therefore, ten regular interradials if the last two small plates above mentioned are to be regarded as interradials. The sutures between the intersecondary radials cannot be distinguished in our specimen, but, from the ornamentation, it is inferred there is one small plate in the first series and two in the second. No azygous area has been determined.

The vault is moderately and evenly convex, with very slightly concave interradial spaces and a small, long subcentral proboscis. It is covered with rather large polygonal plates, the ornamentation of which is destroyed in our specimens. The plates in the interradial areas are elongated and arranged in fan-like order. A horizontal furrow crosses the top of each of the last plates in the calyx, except the minute ones abutting the arm bases, and penetrates the vault at the suture between the plates of the interradial and intersecondary radial areas. Our specimens disclose four of these horizontal elongated passages in each interradial area and two in each secondary interradial area.

A glance at the vault of this species will at once distinguish it from *D. ornatus, D. ornatus var. asperatus* and all other described species. Beside it is remarkable for the comparatively low calyx, broad and deep basal concavity and dense stellate sculpturing of the surface.

Found in the Hamilton Group, at Louisville, Ky., and at Charleston, Indiana, and now in the collection of Wm. F. E. Gurley.

DOLATOCRINUS BULBACEUS n. sp.

Plate II, Fig. 13, basal view; Fig. 14, summit view; Fig. 15, side view.

Calyx and vault together bulbous. Calyx pentagonal from base to the arms, somewhat bowl-shaped, most expanded in the middle part, slightly constricted below the arms; columnar cavity deep. Surface marked by strong radial ridges, and a prominent node in the central part of each first interradial from which radiating ridges extend to the adjoining plates.

Basal plates almost hidden by the column though extending a little beyond it. First primary radials about as long as wide and abruptly bent in the middle, the lower part forming part of the funnel-shaped columnar cavity and the upper end curving as abruptly upward. In the center of each there is a prominent node, from which the radial ridges arise, and which are connected by straight ridges, from one to the other, that form the pentagonal outline of the base, and on which the calyx will rest, if placed on a level surface. Second radials quadrangular, very little wider than high and sides nearly or quite parallel. Third primary radials about twice as wide as high, expanding from below to the lateral angles, pentagonal and supporting upon each of the superior sides two short, secondary radials.

The first secondary radial is much larger and wider than the second and abuts one side against a truncated corner of a first interradial and another against the secondary interradial. The second secondary radials abut against each other, are rounded externally and assume the form of the arms. The arms in each radial series are thus arranged close together, and the arm openings are directed upward. There are only ten arms, and they consist, as we infer from the commencement, of a single series of plates.

The first interradials are the larger plates of the body and have nine sides. They are convex centrally and have a prominent central node from which ridges radiate to adjoining plates. The second interradials are about half as large as the first, bear a central tubercle, are heptagonal, abut laterally upon the first secondary radials, and a small plate that separates the first and secondary radials from the plates of the vault and forms part of the base of the arms, and the two superior sides abut two interradial plates belonging to the vault.

The vault is quite convex, depressed in the interradial areas and bears a subcentral proboscis. It is covered with only a few large, polygonal plates, the surface ornamentation of which is not preserved in either of four specimens examined. There are no pores or passages that penetrate the vault between the arms and there does not seem to be any azygous side.

The general form of this species will readily distinguish it from all others that have been described, but it will be noticed that the number and arrangement of the plates of the calyx is the same as in *D. ornatus* even to the abutting of the second interradials upon the two vault plates, without pores or passages between the arms, though otherwise the vaults are quite different.

Found in the Hamilton Group, at Charleston, Indiana, and now in the collection of Wm. F. E. Gurley.

DOLATOCRINUS VENUSTUS, n. sp.

Plate II, Fig. 16, basal view; Fig. 17, side view; Fig. 18, summit view.

Calyx hemispherical, surface ornamented with radiating ridges and nodes; radial ridges sharp, prominent and interrupted at the sutures. Column large.

Basal plates almost covered by the column. First primary radials wider than long and not extending into the columnar cavity. Second primary radials a little wider than high, quadrangular, sides nearly parallel. Third primary radials a little shorter than the second, pentagonal, expanding to the lateral angles and except two, supporting upon each of the upper sloping sides a single secondary radial; two of them bear four secondary radials each.

Eight of the secondary radials bear upon each upper sloping side three tertiary radials; they grow gradually smaller, and the last ones are followed by cuneiform plates that belong to the arms. There are, therefore, eighteen arms in this species, four in each of three radial series and three in each of the other two series. The arms are composed of a single series of cuneiform plates.

The first interradials are the larger plates of the body and have nine sides. The second interradials are less than half as large as the first and they are each followed by three plates, a small one on each side at the base of the arms and a large one that unites with two plates in the interradial depression on the vault. There seem to be no intersecondary radials. There is no azygous area.

The vault is only slightly convex and moderately depressed in the interradial areas. It bears a long subcental proboscis. It is covered with large polygonal plates that are densely covered with tubercles and short spines. The tubercles are not shown in the illustrations because there are from twenty to fifty on each plate. The two interradial plates in each area that abut upon the last interradial in the calyx are elongated, and the larger plates of the vault. There are no pores or passages that penetrate the vault between the arms.

The hemispherical form and peculiar surface ornamentation distinguish this species. Beside, the number of arms is different from all related species. The number of plates and general order of their arrangement in the calyx, however, are like those in *D. ornatus* and *D. bulbaceus*, notwithstanding the wide variation in the forms of the three species.

Found in the Hamilton Group, at Charleston, Indiana, and now in the collection of Wm. F. E. Gurley.

DOLATOCRINUS AUREATUS n. sp.

Plate III, Fig. 1, basal view; Fig. 2, side view; Fig. 3, summit view.

Calyx hemispherical. Surface ornamented with radiating ridges, usually broken, and nodes; radial ridges sharp and more or less interrupted at the sutures. The sculpturing is more dense than shown in the illustrations. Column round.

Basal plates display a pentagonal rim around the column, where it enters the concavity formed by the basal plates. First primary radials wider than long and abut upon the basal plates without entering the columnar cavity. Second primary radials about twice as wide as long, quadrangular, sides nearly parallel. Third primary radials about half as long as wide, pentagonal, expanding to the lateral angles, and except three, supporting upon each of the upper sloping sides a single secondary radial; three of them bear three secondary radials each.

Seven of the secondary radials bear upon each upper sloping side two tertiary radials, the last one of which is followed by the cuneiform plates that belong to the arms. There are, therefore, seventeen arms in this species, four in each of two radial series and three in each of the other three series. The arms appear to be composed of a single series of cuneiform plates.

The first interradials are the larger plates of the body and have nine sides. The second regular interradials are about half as large as the first and they are each followed by three plates, a small one on each side at the base of the arms and a large one that unites with two large plates in the interradial depression on the vault. There are no intersecondary radials. There is, however, a distinct azygous area shown in our specimen on the side nearest the proboscis. The first and second interradials are like those in the other areas, but the second plate is followed by four or five plates (the sutures are not all distinct), that separate the arms, one-fourth more than they are separated in the other areas, and these unite with three or more plates of the vault, instead of with two as in the other areas.

The vault is moderately convex and depressed in the interradial areas. It bears a long subcentral proboscis on the azygous side. It is covered with large polygonal plates that are densely covered with tubercles. The two interradial plates, in each regular area, that abut upon the last interradial in the calyx, are elongated and the larger plates of the vault. There are no pores or passages that penetrate the vault between the arms.

This species most resembles *D. renustus*, from which it is distinguished by having seventeen instead of eighteen arms, and by having an azygous area. The surface ornamentation, too, is different, but on that ground alone we would not be justified in founding a new species in this genus, for we are satisfied the sculpturing is not uniform on specimens belonging to the same species.

Found in the Hamilton Group, at Charleston, Indiana, and now in the collection of Wm. F. E. Gurley.

DOLATOCRINUS APPROXIMATUS, n. sp.

Plate III, Fig. 4, basal view; Fig. 5, summit view; Fig. 6, side view, showing the three armed radial series.

Calyx bowl-shaped; truncated below; slightly constricted below the arm bases; pentagonal, funnel shaped columnar pit, bounded externally by a raised ridge running from a central tubercle on

—4 G.

each first radial to a central tubercle on the adjacent first radials; column round, perforation small, cinque-foil. Surface ornamented by rather strong radial ridges commencing at the central node on the first primary radials and extending to the arms, and by radiating ridges from a central node on each plate.

Basal plates sunken and so nearly covered by the column as not to be visible externally. First primary radials about as long as wide, one-half the length being in the columnar cavity. Second radials, quadrangular, wider than long, flattened and bearing a prominent central node. Third radials, pentagonal, expanding to the lateral angles, wider than high, four of them bearing upon each upper sloping side four secondary radials and the other one bearing upon one upper sloping side four secondary radials and upon the other a single secondary radial which bears upon each of the upper sloping sides three tertiary radials. Four of the radial series thus bear two arms each and the other bears three arms, making eleven arms in this species. From the arm bases it might be inferred that the arms are composed of a double series of interlocking plates, as there are two plates at the base instead of one, but two furrows are not seen to enter the vault.

First interradials the larger plates of the calyx and have nine sides. Second interradials less than half as large as the first, hexagonal, and support three small plates in the third range, which are followed by three smaller plates that separate the arm bases and unite with the plates of the vault. Intersecondary radials two, separating the arm bases and uniting with the plates of the vault. No azygous side.

Vault moderately convex, with a subcentral proboscis and composed of convex polygonal plates. Those in the interradial areas are elongated and disposed in a fan-like arrangement. Four pores or passages enter the vault in each interradial area, and two in each intersecondary area; they are continued by a shallow furrow across the top of the last range of interradials.

This species is more nearly related to *D. lacus* than to any other that has been described. It is distinguished, however, by having eleven arms instead of ten, which, alone, we regard as of specific importance. It is further distinguished by having one more secondary radial and one more interradial in the third range, which we think is of specific importance, especially as our specimen is much smaller than any specimen of *D. lacus* we have seen. The difference in size and in surface ornamentation we do not regard as of importance, especially where, as in this case, the two species have the same general form and without careful examination might be taken one for the other. A basal view of the two species is alike.

Found in the Hamilton Group, at Louisville, Ky., and now in the collection of Wm. F. E. Gurley.

DOLATOCRINUS LINEOLATUS, n. sp.

Plate III, Fig. 7, basal view; Fig. 8, side view; Fig. 9, summit view, the small plates near the arm openings are not distinguished.

Calyx hemispherical, very slightly constricted below the arm bases, which protrude nearly horizontally. Surface ornamented with fine radiating lines, in fascicles of three, that run from a sharp prominent node, in the center of each principal plate, to the central node in each adjacent plate. Radial ridges small, sharp, continuous over the sutures and bearing a sharp node at the center of each plate. Column round, rather small.

Basal plates almost covered by the column. First primary radials a little wider than long and not extending into the columnar cavity. Second primary radials about twice as wide as long, quadrangular, sides nearly parallel. Third primary radials longer and wider than the second; about twice as wide as long; expanding to the lateral angles, pentagonal and bearing upon the upper sloping sides the secondary radials. One of them bears upon each upper sloping side three secondary radials and each of the other four bear upon one upper sloping side three secondary radials and upon the other one a single pentagonal secondary radial that bears upon each upper sloping side two tertiary radials. There are, therefore, three arms to each of four radial series and two arms to the other one, making fourteen arms in all. The arm bases project nearly horizontally. The arms are composed of a single series of cuneiform plates.

The first interradials are the larger plates of the body and have nine sides. The second interradials are more than half as large as the first and reach to the summit of the calyx. This plate in the second range is followed by three plates, the central one is the larger and unites with two plates on the vault and the lateral ones form part of the arm bases. There are no intersecondary radials. There is no azygous area.

The vault is quite convex and much depressed in the interradial areas, which is made more conspicuous by the prominence of the ambulacral areas, at the base of the arms. There is a long subcentral proboscis. The vault is covered with large polygonal plates; the smaller plates over the arm furrows near the openings in the vault are not shown in the illustrations, because the sutures are not distinct in our specimens. It is rare that they are correctly exhibited in illustrations of other species, for the same reason. The plates are covered with tubercles, those near the base of the proboscis being somewhat spinous. The two interradial plates, in each area, that abut upon the three plates in the third range of interradials belonging to the calyx, are elongated and the larger plates of the vault. There are no pores or passages that penetrate the vault between the arms.

This species is distinguished by its general form, surface ornamentation and by having fourteen arms. It is probably as nearly related to *D. venustus* as to any other species.

Found in the Hamilton Group, at Charleston, Indiana, and now in the collection of Wm. F. E. Gurley.

DOLATOCRINUS GREENEI, n. sp.

Plate III, Fig. 10, basal view; Fig. 11, side view; Fig. 12, summit view.

Calyx hemispherical, very slightly constricted below the arm bases. Surface sculptured in a variety of ways; there are prominent nodes in the central part of the larger plates from which there are radiating ridges and there are shorter radiating ridges that do not arise from the central nodes, beside scattering tubercles. The radiating ridges are interrupted at the sutures and ventricose in the middle part of the plates with a node at the center of each. Column round, medium size.

Basal plates expose a pentagonal rim around the column. First primary radials wider than long and of unequal size, two of them, on the azygous side, being much larger than the others, as shown in the upper part of Figure 10. Second primary radials only slightly wider than long, quadrangular, sides nearly parallel. Third primary radials, about the same length as the second, expand to the lateral angles, and bear upon each upper sloping side, except one, a single secondary radial. Upon one side of the radial series opposite the azygous side there are three secondary radials, the last one of which bears a cuneiform arm plate. The first secondary radials are large and bear upon each upper sloping side two tertiary radials. There are, therefore, four arms to each of four radial series and three arms in the radial series opposite the azygous area, making nineteen arms in this species. The arm bases are not large and the arms appear to be composed of a single series of cuneiform plates.

The first interradials are the larger plates of the body and have nine sides, in three of the areas; but, in the other two areas, there are two interradial plates in the first range and together they are much larger than the single first interradials. The two interradials in the first range in the two areas may be seen to abut upon the two large first primary radials in Figure 10, one plate extending below the other and one of them may be seen on the left of Figure 11. We cannot say that the two large first primary radials, followed laterally by two plates, in the first range of interradials, represent an abnormal development. We have only one specimen. The two first primary radials are substantially alike and the two peculiar interradial areas are substantially alike. If they are abnormal there is regularity about them, and they are each separated by a four-armed radial series from the three-armed series. There is only one plate in the second range, in three of the areas, and two in the other two areas. In the third range there are three plates, the central one is the larger and unites with two plates on the vault and the lateral ones form part of the arm bases. There are no intersecondary radials. There is an azygous side if we would embrace within it two radial series and three interradial areas, but there cannot be said to be a single azygous area as that term is applied in the description of crinoids.

The vault is only slightly convex but rather strongly depressed in the interradial areas between the arm bases. There is a small subcentral proboscis. The vault is covered with rather large polygonal plates, the two, in the interradial areas that abut upon the plates in the third range of the interradials, are elongated and the larger plates of the vault. All the plates bear tubercles and a few of them bear a central spine each that is surrounded with tubercles. There are no pores or passages that penetrate the vault between the arms.

This species is distinguished by its wide calyx, low vault, peculiar form, surface ornamentation and number of arms.

Found in the Hamilton Group, at Louisville, Ky., by G. K. Greene, in whose honor the specific name is proposed, and now in the collection of S. A. Miller.

Remarks.—We have described and illustrated fourteen species of *Dolatocrinus*, being all that are now known from Ohio, Indiana and Kentucky. Eleven of these are new to science, one of the others has never before been figured, and the other two are illustrated and redescribed for the purpose of showing characters not heretofore known. We call attention to the fact that no one has discovered an azygous opening in any of the species, and this important character or part of the ordinary structure of crinoids may fairly be said not to exist in this genus. *D. magnificus* and *D. aurealus* have each an azygous side to the calyx and vault and *D. greenei* has two azygous areas in the calyx, while none of the other species have an azygous side or azygous area.

D. grandis, D. lacus, D. marshi, D. stellifer and *D. approximatus* have orifices entering the body through the vault, between the arms, an important structure having no existence in *D. magnificus, D. ornatus, D. ornatus var. asperatus, D. bulbaceus, D. venustus, D. aurealus, D. lincolatus* or *D. greenei*, and whether or not the character belongs to *D. spinosus* is not determined. These orifices, though conspicuous in the species to which they belong, have not, so far as we are advised, been heretofore mentioned, and it would seem, therefore, appropriate for us to state more fully the structure and appearance and the possible or probable physiological functions with which they were connected.

We regard them as excurrent orifices for the reason that they cross the plates of the calyx at the summit by a furrow and enter the vault horizontally, which is inconsistent with any other hypothesis. What flowed through the orifices flowed through the channels across the thickness of the plates of the calyx, for we cannot conceive of any other utility or purpose of the furrows. Nothing could have flowed through the furrows and entered the orifices for the purpose of gaining access to the interior of the body, for there was no means of propelling anything in that direction. Endosmosis would not take place in that way.

They may have been used as conduits for the waste material that entered through the ambulacral furrows, or for the discharge of surplus water, but whatever their purpose they must have been used in the performance of some important physiological function. There would seem to be no doubt of that fact. This conclusion leads us to ask why, if they were so important to the species possessing them, did the greater number of species in the genus exist without them? The question is unanswered and at present unanswerable, because the physiological functions performed, at the seat of life, which is supposed to have been near the central part and on a level with the top of the calyx, in this genus of palaeozoic crinoids, are not known. The orifices are elongated externally and in their passage through the vault, because they are directed horizontally through the convex vault, and the elongation, therefore, depends upon the convexity of the vault in the different species.

CRINOID BASES.

Plate III, Fig. 13, superior side of an eroded base: Fig. 14, inferior side of same.

Crinoid bases are as full of pores as sponges and, when silicified, they may be cleaned with acid and made to expose the pores as shown in the illustrations. Weathered specimens, when not silicified, expose the pores, and a broken fragment will expose them also. Unaltered and finely preserved specimens do not expose the pores externally. The column is inserted in an obconoidal cavity in the base and the pores radiate from this cavity in all directions to the farthest extremities of the base. They are rarely larger than an ordinary sewing needle, and generally less in size, but so numerous that the interspaces have a diameter but little more than the diameter of the pores. The radiating pores are more or less sinuous and accommodated to the irregularities of the base.

These pores, as we suppose, were connected with the columnar canal and through them the material passed that formed the base. The histogenesis of the base may be compared with the formation and development of the bones of an animal. The mucous or fluid substance, that contained the material for the base, passed through the columnar canal into the pores of the base and was deposited iu a softer state than it afterward assumed. In this way the base increased in size with the growth of the animal, and was made to fill the inequalities of the surface, to which it attached, and to extend over the border so as to form hooks or anchors of support. The nutrition for the formation of the organic structure of the base was furnished in the same manner that it was supplied for all other parts of the skeleton of a crinoid. The pores of the base were channels for nutrition and were appropriated exclusively to the construction and support of it.

The plates of a crinoid column were enlarged with the growth of the animal, as bones and shells are increased in size; but new plates seem to have originated exclusively at the lower end, or within the obconoidal cavity, in the base, at the end of the column; none appear to have been intercalated between older plates and none were added at the superior end of the column. The columnar canal was, therefore, a channel for nutrition, and nothing passed into it except the digested and reparatory juices' for the columnar cords or tendons and the skeletal plates and base.

The base illustrated is from the Hamilton Group, at Louisville, Ky., but it does not differ in organic texture or structure from bases found in other groups of rocks.

FAMILY ICHTHYOCRINIDAE.

LECANOCRINUS OSWEGOENSIS n. sp.

Plate III, Fig. 15, view on the right of the ray on the azygous side; Fig. 16, azygous side; Fig. 17, view of the ray between the azygous area and the area shown in Fig. 15, and which bears four primary radials.

Species small, subelliptical in general outline. Calyx obconoidal, bulged on the right of the azygous area, truncated for a small, round column, which is composed of thin plates, exposing the serrated edges for the union of the plates, and having a very small columnar canal. Plates of the calyx slightly convex and covered with granules: sutures distinct.

The three basals form a low pentagonal cup, about twice the diameter of the column. The subradials are of unequal size, the one below the azygous area is the larger and has seven sides, two of the others are hexagonal and two pentagonal. There are four primary radials in the series on the right of the azygous area and three in each of the other series. The first primary radials are unequal in size, the one on the right of the azygous area being the smaller and having only five sides, the others are hexagonal or heptagonal, depending upon whether they are truncated upon one or both superior lateral angles by the first interradials. The second primary radials are short and wide and of very unequal size, the one on the right of the azygous area is the larger and is hexagonal, the others are subquadrangular, but when a superior lateral angle is truncated by a second interradial they become pentagonal. Four of the third primary radials are short, wide, pentagonal and bear upon the upper sloping sides the secondary radials or free arms; the other third primary radial is short, wide, subquadrangular though slightly truncated at the superior lateral

—5 G.

angle on the azygous side, so as to make it pentagonal; and it is then followed by a fourth primary radial which is pentagonal and axillary, and bears upon the upper sloping side the secondary radials or free arms. The arms preserved in our specimen have three short, secondary radials, in each, the last one of which is pentagonal and supports, on each upper sloping side, a third series of plates.

There are two small regular interradials in each area, one above the other; the first one separates the second and third primary radials, in each series, in some of the areas, it truncates the superior angles of the first primary radials, in others it does not extend so low. The first azygous plate is rather larger than the first primary radial on the right and has eight sides; it truncates a subradial, abuts upon three primary radials on the right, though the third one truncates the angle only slightly, two on the left, and is followed by two plates on the superior side, the one on the left being quite small. The larger plate in the second range is succeeded by a small plate on the right, which is all that is preserved in our specimen, but the facet for another plate in the middle part is well preserved. The azygous area, therefore, has five or more plates.

This species is readily distinguished from all others by the general form, regular interradial plates, azygous interradials and series of four primary radials in one of the rays. It is wholly unnecessary to compare it with any of them, though it clearly belongs to this genus.

Found in the Niagara Group, at Oswego, Illinois, and now in the collection of Wm. F. E. Gurley.

Family **ACTINOCRINIDAE.**

MEGISTOCRINUS EXPANSUS n. sp.

Plate III, Fig. 18, basal view of a large specimen; Fig. 19, summit view of the same; Fig. 20, side view of the same; Fig. 21, basal view of a small specimen showing the commencement of the horizontal arms.

Calyx very shallow; broadly basin-shaped; from three to five times as wide as high; columnar cavity, evenly concave, commencing from about the middle of the second radials, the superior part of which curve upward; the calyx continues to expand from the second radials to the arms, expanding more rapidly as the arms are approached. The arms are directed horizontally. The column is round and of medium size. The vault is one-half higher than the calyx and has twice the capacity.

The basal plates have an hexagonal outline, about one-half wider than the diameter of the column. The first primary radials abutting on a single basal plate are hexagonal, those abutting on two basals are heptagonal. The second primary radials are a little larger than the first and hexagonal. The third primary radials are about the size of the first, pentagonal, and support upon each upper sloping side secondary radials.

The external surfaces of all the plates covering the three specimens at hand, one of them being intermediate in size between the two illustrated, are more or less eroded or disintegrated. The best preserved plates are beveled at the sutures, and it is, therefore, believed that specimens having a well preserved external surface will show distinctly the outlines of all the plates. In our specimens the sutures of the secondary and tertiary radials and those of the vault are generally obscure; some of them are, however, distinct. This is the reason the illustrations are not made to show all the plates, and, for the same reason, there is a little doubt about the number and shape of some of the plates just below the top of the calyx.

The first secondary radials are nearly as large as the third primary radials. In one of the lateral rays on each side there are no tertiary radials. In each of these two rays the second secondary radials are somewhat smaller than the first and extend to the lower part of the commencement of the enlargement for the arms. There are three or four more plates in each series, forming the base of the arms, before the arms become free. This gives us five or six secondary radials in each series, and two arms to each of these rays. In the other three rays there is only a single secondary radial in each. It is pentagonal and supports upon each of the upper sloping sides tertiary radials. There are four or five tertiary radials in each series, the last three or four of which form the base of the arms before they become free. The last two or three plates in each of the radial series are more or less cuneiform before the arms become free. There are, therefore, four arms to each of three rays and two arms to each of the other two rays, making in all sixteen arms to this species. The arms are composed of a single series of cuneiform plates.

In the interradial areas there is one hexagonal plate separating the second primary radials, and two plates in the second range separating the third primary radials, each of which is about the size of the primary radials. There are three plates in the third range, three in the fourth and three in the fifth; the last form a sharp ridge between the arm bases, which rises above the vault plates, that abut against it. In the intersecondary areas there is one plate in the first range and two in the second; the latter form a sharp ridge between the arm bases, which rises above the vault plates that abut against it. First azygous plate in line with the first primary radials and of the same size; it is followed by three plates of the same size as the first radials. Above these the area and arrangement of the plates is very much like the regular areas, with about one more plate in each range.

The vault bears a large central plate with a big conical spine. There is also a spinous plate over the junction of the ambulacral furrows in each series, making six spinous plates on the vault. The plates that cover the vault are polygonal and of very unequal size. There is an orifice on the azygous side of the central spine. The ambulacral areas are raised into rounded ridges and the interradial areas are depressed between the arms. The surface of the plates, in our specimens, is destroyed and the larger number of the sutures are not discernable.

This species is distinguished, by its general form, from all others. The broad shallow calyx, high convex vault, and horizontal arms will alone distinguish it. The number and arrangement of the arms is also a distinguishing feature as well as the surface of the plates, for most species from rocks of the same geological age, have highly convex or subspinous plates in the calyx.

Found in the Hamilton Group, at Louisville, Ky., and now in the collections of the authors.

AN INTERESTING LETTER.

There is a letter, on file in the State Museum of Natural History of Illinois, belonging to the Geological Department, from Charles Wachsmuth, dated, at Burlington, Iowa, August 9, 1892, containing the following paragraph:

"I have described the *Eucalyptocrinus lindahli* and have sent the description, together with that of some other new species from the Niagara Group to the American Geologist for early publication, to secure priority, as I am aware that S. A. Miller will be out this fall, on some of the same species. This, of course, is confidential, for I do not want Miller to know it."

There was no more sympathizing place, for the publication of such material, than the American Geologist, a journal that never aspires to a higher level in scientific matters.

PLATE 1

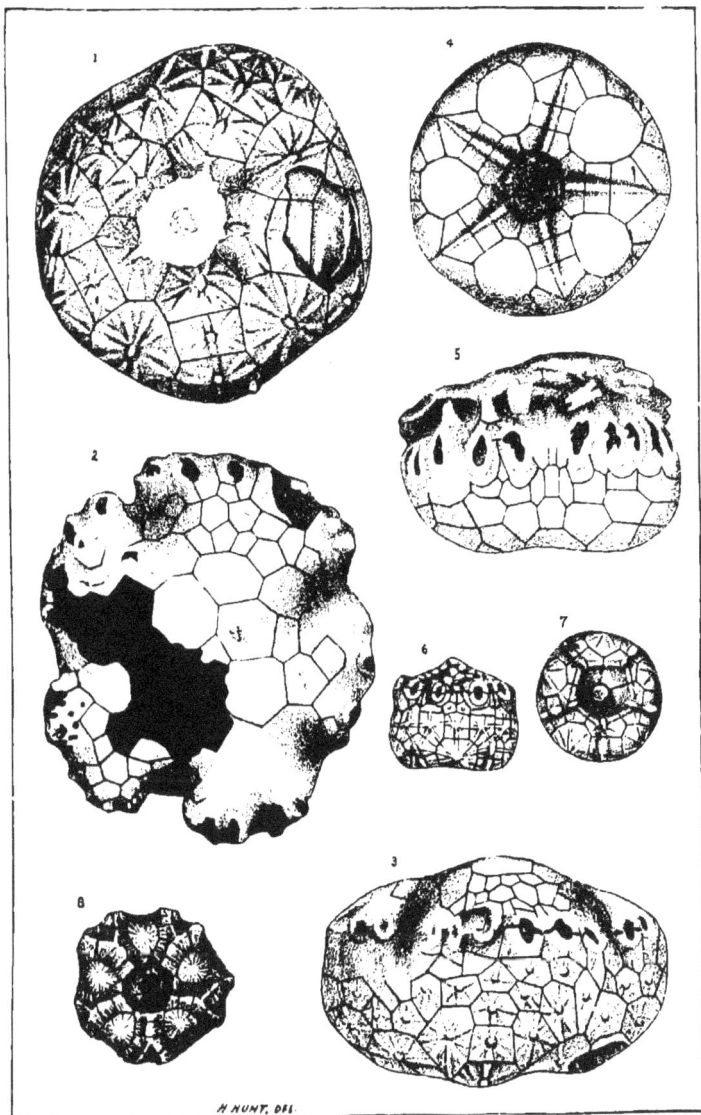

` PLATE II.

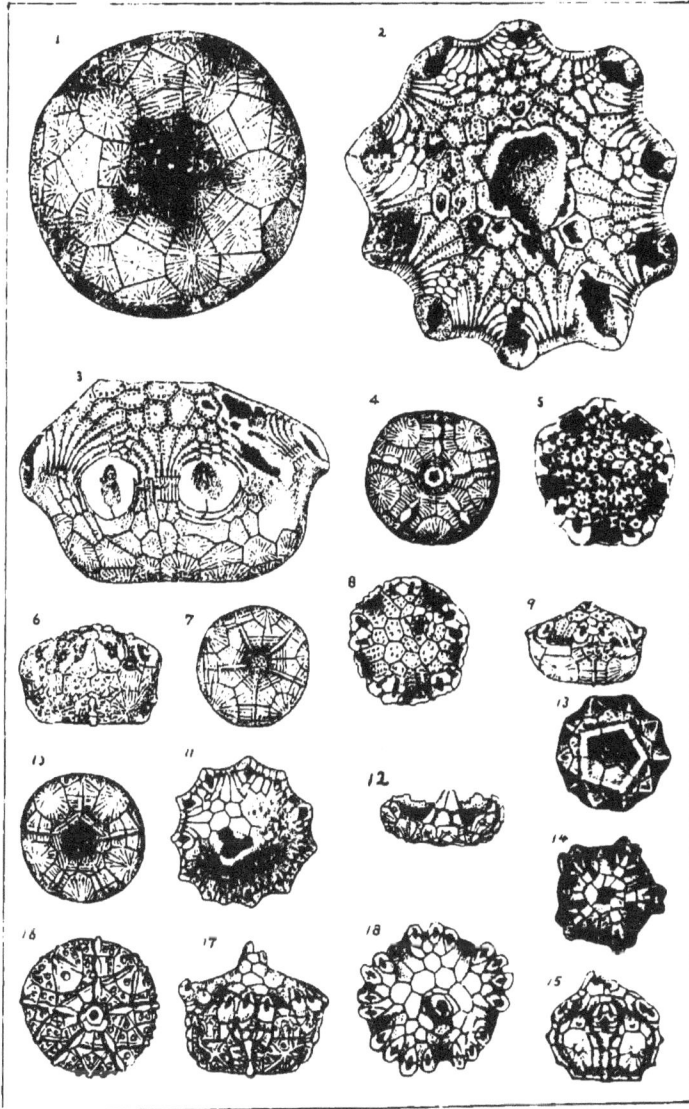

PLATE III.

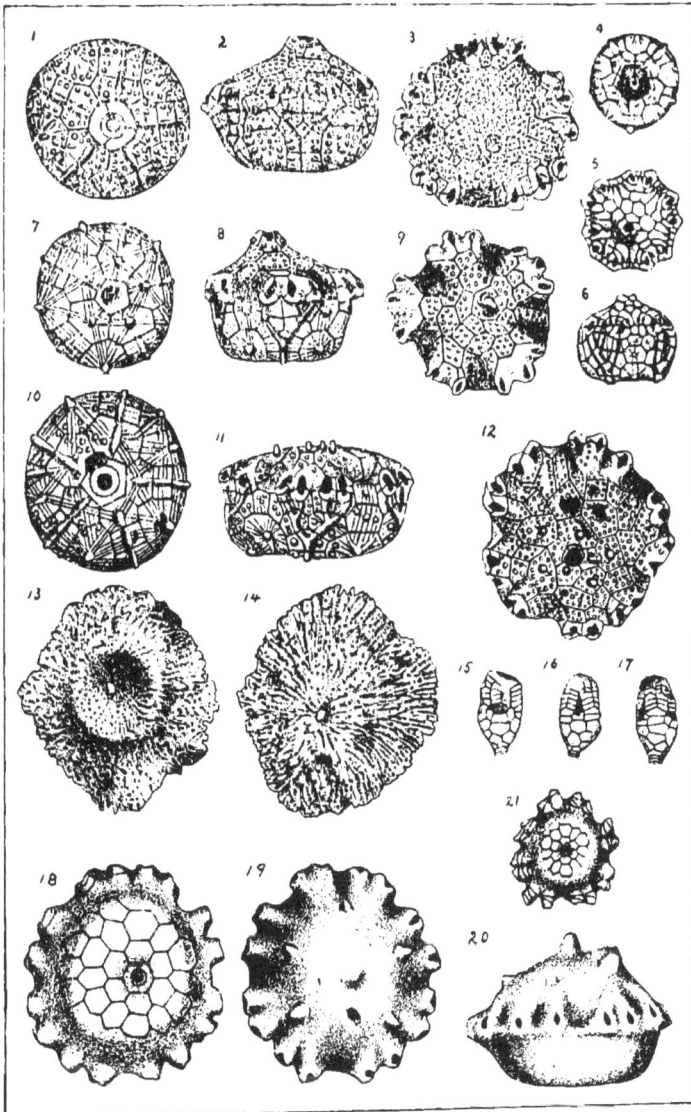

www.ingramcontent.com/pod-product-compliance
Lightning Source LLC
Chambersburg PA
CBHW032033090426
42733CB00031B/875